Panorama-Books: BARBADOS

With thirty color plates

HANS W. HANNAU

BARBADOS

ANDERMANN PUBLISHERS

Wrapper and cover designed by Gerhard M. Hotop

Dedicated to independant Barbados
and my dear friends there, with my best wishes.
HANS HANAU

Library of Congress Catalog Card No. 67–12655
Wilhelm Andermann Verlag, Munich
Printed in Germany. 166

Barbados has an enchantment all its own, which has proved irresistible to thousands of travelers. The perfect year-round climate, the peaceful atmosphere, the excellent hotels and other accommodations, the picturesque scenery both coastal and inland, and, last but not least, the friendliness and charm of the people contribute vastly to the enjoyment of Barbados. The hospitality seems inborn: the Barbadians welcome visitors sincerely and concern themselves with their comfort – making newcomers feel quickly at home.

Of course, there are the superb facilities for sports lovers: fine golf courses, tennis courts, polo fields, horse racing, and unequaled fishing. Barbados is the "Island of the Flying Fish," and sailfish, dolphin kingfish, albacore, and many other challenging varieties abound as well.

A BIT OF ENGLAND IN THE TROPICS

Barbados is one of the happiest little islands in the Caribbean. It has been described as an English garden transplanted to the tropics, for it is English to the core. The quiet, cultivated countryside resembles the mother country's southern shires, Devon and Kent, with their rolling hills, bowers, and patchwork of carefully tended fields.

Many of the British West Indian islands at one time or another were ruled by France or Spain or Holland – or even in succession by all three. But Barbados, ever since it was colonized in 1627 by the English, has owed allegiance to England alone and has adhered to the patterns of English life. As a consequence, English traditions are stronger in Barbados than elsewhere in the Caribbean. Cricket playing, horse racing, polo, high tea, and English orderliness and fair play are typical of the Barbadian social and civic patterns. Anglican village churches and such English place names as Yorkshire, Windsor, and Hastings contribute to the tone of Barbados. In Bridgetown there is a Trafalgar Square dominated by a statue of Lord Nelson that antedates the London statue by 27 years.

Animal
Flowercave

BARBADOS

St.
Lucy

Pico
Teneriffe

St. Peter

ATLANTIC
OCEAN

Speights-
Town

St.
Andrew

CARIBBEAN
SEA

St.
Thomas

St.
James

Bathseba

Conset
Bay

St.
Joseph

Codrington
College

Hole
Town

St. John

Ragged
Point

St.
George

Deep Water
Harbor

St. Philip

Sam
Lords - Castle

Crane
Beach

Bridgetown

St.
Michael

Christ

Carlisle Bay

Church

Hastings
St. Lawrence

Airport

Oistins Bay

Before the English arrived, the Arawak Indians were there. Their weapons and tools, made of shells, are still being discovered in caves and along the seashore. In 1536 a Portuguese explorer, Pedro a Campos, left some hogs to breed, so that a supply of fresh meat might be available to him on further journeys. Sixteenth-century maps give the island's name as Bernardo, and while the history of its present name is obscure, "Barbados" is probably a corruption of the Portuguese or Spanish barbudos ("bearded"), a word descriptive of the configuration of the fig trees dotting the island.

When a vessel under the command of Captain John Powell entered Barbadian waters in 1625, the island was deserted. The Arawaks had either been driven away by the fierce and warlike Caribs on a raiding expedition or enslaved by the Spanish to work the mines of Hispaniola. On a tree at the site of his landing, Powell inscribed the words "James K. of E. and of this island." Two years later the first British colonists cleared the land around the tree and created the settlement of Jamestown, later called Holetown but more popularly known as St. James, at a point midway between Harrison Point and Carlisle Bay on the west coast. (Today, this is one of the finest resort districts on the island.)

During the long wars for supremacy over the Caribbean, Barbados was a tempting morsel for conquering European countries. To protect it against being swallowed, Barbados was turned by the English into a fortress, at one time containing twenty-one forts spaced along twenty-one miles of coastline. Despite the island's determined efforts to keep warring powers and other marauders away, Captain Kidd landed in Payne's Bay, according to legend, and buried his treasure there, only six miles from Bridgetown. A chart showing the site has been discovered, but the treasure has not. Hopeful treasure hunters still search for it.

Under the plantation system, the island prospered. Negro slaves were imported to work the sugar cane fields after this crop was introduced from Brazil in the early seventeenth century. Relatively humane treatment of the slave population spared Barbados the horrible and bloody slave insurrections known on other West Indian islands. Slavery was abolished in 1834.

A NEW NATION

On November 30, 1966, the people of Barbados assumed responsibility for their own destiny. After a constitutional conference in London in June 1966, the island became independent, having its own democratic government and its own flag, national anthem, and coat of arms.

Barbados had enjoyed one of the oldest constitutional and representative systems in the Commonwealth. Its House of Assembly dates back to 1639, and the creation of an Executive Committee in 1881 was the beginning of ministerial government, which was completed by 1954. The party system was introduced in 1946, and complete internal self-government came in October 1961. One step further, independence, brought to Barbados the full right to conduct its own international affairs as an independent nation within the British Commonwealth.

Barbados has an area of 166 square miles – measuring 21 miles from north to south and a scant 14 miles from east to west. The island is the most easterly of the Lesser Antilles, jutting far out into the Atlantic, 95 miles due east of St. Vincent, 200 miles northeast of Trinidad, and 600 miles southeast of San Juan, Puerto Rico. This coral-capped island, with its beautiful pink-and-white coral-sand beaches, has no real rivers – but there is a plentiful underground water supply.

The great charm of the island is its scenic variety, both urban and rural. Hills and dales, coves and beaches, sugar cane fields and palm trees, donkey carts, limousines and jet airplanes, towns and villages that seem to have stepped out of an earlier century are all part of it. The highest point is Mount Hillaby, in the north-central area, which rises to a height of 1100 feet. Roads are narrow but well surfaced, winding from village to village much as in rural England. The climate is delightful and the island enjoys the natural air-conditioning of sea breezes. One can count on the fingers of one's hand the number of days that the sun does not shine. Once known as "The sanatorium of the West Indies," Barbados is particularly blessed with clear, fresh air and a peaceful, unhurried way of life that works wonders toward restoring mental tranquility and physical well-being.

POPULATION

The 1963 census recorded a population of 240.468 – or 1460 to the square mile. The majority are of African origin, a few are European, and the balance are of diverse ancestry. The island is almost devoid of Orientals.

FLORA AND FAUNA

Long ago, Barbados was a wilderness of forests and dense copses. Many adventurers, in rebellion against the Civil Wars in England, set sail for Barbados. They soon found the enormous growth an almost insurmountable obstacle in their cultivation of the land for food crops. Numbering a few thousand and abetted by many Negroes, they cleared most of the land for sugar plantations and other foods, for export and their own consumption. Today, except for two or three areas, the forests are gone.

There are few wild animals on Barbados. In the remaining forests there are some noisy monkeys, but most of the island presents a familiar assortment of domestic animals – cows and chickens, dogs and cats, and the usual farm animals. Rarely, one spots a playful raccoon or a timid hare.

Among the awe-inspiring sights on the island are the casuarina trees, which often reach a height of one hundred and fifty feet, their topmost branches wafted to and fro by the tropical breezes. Then there are the cabbage palms, rising to a hundred feet, the ebony trees with sweet-smelling, colorful buds in early spring, coconut palms in profusion, sand-box trees, calabashes – and the bearded fig trees. The island also has great displays of ferns, sea grapes, delicious red berries, and many forms of cactus.

Barbados is a bird lover's paradise. Many species are native to the area, and during the winter season others add song and color.

INDUSTRIES

Basically, the island is dependent on its farming, principally sugar cane, with its by-products of rum and molasses, the revenue from which provides many essential imports. And, as is the situation in most Caribbean islands today, tourism ranks second, attracting approximately 75,000 visitors a year, and the figure is growing rapidly.

Other industries, most of them comparatively new, produce candles, pottery, electric batteries, paints, beverages, furniture, chemicals, drugs, food products, clothing, and detergents.

DEEP-WATER HARBOR

Recently completed (1961) at a cost of $ 30,000,000 and four years' labor, Bridgetown's deep-water harbor can now accommodate eight large ships at one time in its mammoth berthing facilities, thereby ending an age of cargo lighters and passenger tenders and inaugurating an era in which Barbados becomes an important area in world shipping and a favorite port of call for cruise ships.

There are here, as well, three tremendous storage areas, and a Customs Department, a Free-port Shop, and an Information Bureau.

Three loading towers discharge sugar, the mainstay of the Barbados economy, into ships at a rate of 500 tons an hour. The deep-water harbor handles 400,000 tons of cargo annually, of which 160,000 tons is sugar.

Should you come to Barbados by plane, you will cross Carlisle Bay and the undulating green hills around it, so reminiscent of England's midland country. Gliding into Seawell Airport, the plane dips over the pounding surf. A half-moon of ice-cream-colored houses lines the bay, which leads into the harbor and Careenage of Bridgetown, the capital.

In the Careenage, tall-masted schooners from all over the Caribbean crowd the narrow strip of water within the inlet. The docks are filled with sailors, visitors, shoppers, and "higglers" (peddlers).

The brilliantly colored sails and the brightly clad populace milling about the docks provide an impression of what life was like here during Nelson's time. Even the Barbados Harbor Police, clad in bell-bottom trousers, white pullover middies with triangular kerchief, and flat boaters with black bands, wear the uniform of Nelson's sailors. Regular Barbados policemen in immaculate white jackets and blue trousers with crimson side stripe can be seen directing the heavy traffic of automobiles, donkey carts, pushcarts, and trucks.

13

At the center of the Old City of Bridgetown (population about 40,000) is a landmark for travelers – the bronze statue of Lord Nelson in Trafalgar Square, of which the Barbadians, or Bajans, as they prefer to call themselves, are very proud. Grateful sugar planters erected the statue as a thanks offering to the Admiral for breaking Napoleon's continental blockade and so protecting their foreign markets.

Broad Street is the shopping center of the island. Here one can obtain wooden replicas of women selling Mauby (a soft drink), the Harbor Police, and other well-known Barbadian types. Luxury items imported from all over the world, particularly from the British Isles, are sold here duty-free.

Nearby are the neo-Gothic Public Buildings, which contain fine specimens of stained-glass windows imported from England. Inside are the chambers of the Senate and House of Assembly, with their stained-glass-window representations of England's rulers from James I to Queen Victoria.

A colorful local handicraft center is Pelican Village, near the Bridgetown Harbor. In the city a war memorial honors the Barbadians who died in World Wars I and II.

The first St. Michael's Cathedral was built in 1665; the present building dates from 1831 and is built of coral rock. A history of colonial days can be read in the memorial tablets, which go back to the seventeenth century. Here George Washington came to worship in 1751. At the age of nineteen, he undertook to accompany his brother, Lawrence, to Barbados. Lawrence was suffering from tuberculosis and it was thought that the warm, healthful climate of Barbados would help him. There is a house on Upper Bay Street called Washington House where, it is said, the brothers lived. Smallpox was prevalent at the time, and George caught a mild case of it, which immunized him against the far more serious and virulent ravages of the disease that was to despoil the Revolutionary troops. The pit marks on his face were caught by Stuart in his famous portrait of the first president of the United States.

Washington loved the island. He wrote that he was "perfectly enraptured with the beautiful prospects . . . on every side the fields of cane, corn, fruit trees in a delightful green setting."

A mile and a half out of town is the excellent Barbados Museum, where old maps, prints, coins, Indian artifacts, and exhibits of Barbadian fauna provide an interesting survey of the island's history and natural beauties.

Sam Lord's Castle stands fourteen miles from the capital on the southeast end of the island. Built by Sam Lord in 1830, this was one of the Great Estate Houses of Barbados. The white stone building, nestled in beautiful gardens, is really a castle. The furnishings are priceless antiques. The original owner, the story goes, was a cruel man who occasionally locked his wife in the castle dungeon and maneuvered more than one vessel into wrecking itself on the rocky reefs by hanging lanterns that resembled the lights of safely harbored ships. Today Sam Lord's Castle is a highly distinguished and popular resort. The master bedroom still has Sam's own great mahogany four-poster bed. There are excellent paintings by Bartolomeo, Lely, Raeburn, Reynolds, and Zucarelli.

Codrington College, a seminary, is on the east coast along the drive north of Sam Lord's Castle. It is completely English in appearance and spirit and reminds one of Oxford, in spite of the palm trees. It is the oldest college in the British West Indies, dating from 1716.

St. John's Church, to the north, is eight hundred feet above sea level and dates from the seventeenth century. It offers a breathtaking panorama of the magnificent windward coast. Its quiet and very English churchyard contains the tomb of Ferdinando Paleologus, whose family ruled as Emperors in Constantinople.

The drive along the windward or Atlantic coast is truly spectacular. The plunging cliffs and turbulent surf are similar to what one will find in Cornwall, England. Proceeding inland, you will come to Barbados' rugged Scotland District, where the "Redlegs" live. "Redleg" is a term originating in England to describe a kilted, bare-legged Scotsman. The "Redlegs" are the blonde, blue-eyed descendants of early indentured white servants who were sold into slavery after an unsuccessful rebellion against James II of England.

Mahogany and casuarina trees adorn the landscape. Occasionally you will sight a wild monkey or two gamboling from tree to tree. Old windmills, once used for grinding sugar cane, give evidence of the still-prosperous sugar industry. Farley Hill, now a complete ruin, was built in the eighteenth century. The house was used in the filming of Hollywood's Island in the Sun.

The road west across the island from Farley Hill leads directly to Speightstown, Barbados' second main town, on the leeward side of the island. The coast here is washed by the placid waters of the Caribbean and is the "Riviera" of Barbados. The tranquil shoreline contrasts sharply with the wilder, more rugged windward coast. Relatively uncluttered with resorts, because wealthy Americans, Canadians, and Englishmen prefer to have it that way, it contains, nevertheless, a wide variety of hotels and inns ranging from the very modest to the downright luxurious.

Carlisle Bay
ans la baie de Carlisle
der Carlisle-Bucht
bahía de Carlisle

Old Sugar Mill
Ancienne sucrerie
Alte Zuckerrohrmühle
Viejo molino azucarero

Bridgetown.
The Careenage

Bridgetown.
Le Carénage

Bridgetown.
Careenage

Bridgetown.
El carenero

Secluded Beach on the Caribbean Coast (Eastry House)
Plage retirée sur la côte caribienne (Eastry House)
Versteckter Strand an der Karibischen Küste bei Eastry House
Playa solitaria en la costa del Caribe (Eastry House)

St. James Coast at Coral Reef Club
La côte Saint-Jacques avec le Coral Reef Club
Die St.-James-Küste beim Coral-Reef-Klub
Costa de St. James y Club de Arrecifes de Coral

Welchman's Hall Gully

Garrison Race Track
Course de chevaux
à Garrison
Rennbahn
von Garrison
Hipódromo
de Garrison

The old Harbor of Speightstown (St. Peter's)
Le vieux port de Speightstown (Saint-Pierre)
Der alte Hafen von Speightstown (St. Peter)
El viejo puerto de Speightstown (St. Peter)

*St. Michael's Cathedral,
Bridgetown*

*La Cathédrale Saint-Michel
à Bridgetown*

*St.-Michaels-Kathedrale,
Bridgetown*

*La Catedral de San Miguel,
en Bridgetown*

Atlantic Coast at Bathsheba
La côte atlantique à Bathsheba
Atlantikküste bei Bathsheba
La costa atlántica en Bathsheba

Sugar-Cane Fields on the Eastern Slopes from Cherry Tree Hill
Champs de canne à sucre sur les versants orientaux
Zuckerrohrfelder an der Ostküste, Blick von Cherry Tree Hill
Plantaciones de caña de azúcar en la vertiente oriental

Rockley Golf Course
Terrain de golf à Rockley
Rockley-Golfplatz
Campo de golf de Rockley

Paradise Beach at Freshwater Bay (St. James)
La Plage du Paradis à Freshwater Bay (Saint-Jacques)
Der Paradiesstrand an der Freshwater-Bucht (St. James)
Playa paradisíaca en la bahía de Freshwater (St. James)

Barbados International Airport
and the Police Force
L'aéroport international
de Barbados
et le corps de police
Paradierende Polizei
auf dem internationalen
Flughafen
Fuerzas de policía
en el aeropuerto internacional
de Barbados

The Marine Hotel, a Historic
Landmark
Le Marine Hotel, un point
de repère historique
Das Marine Hotel, ein
historisches Wahrzeichen
El Hotel Marina, que constituye
un mojón histórico

<

North Point
near Animal Flower Cave
North Point
près d'Animal Flower Cave
North Point
bei Animal Flower Cave
North Point
en el Animal Flower Cave

St. Martin's Church
L'église Saint-Martin
St.-Martins-Kirche
Iglesia de San Martín

Beach at Sandy Lane (St. James)
La plage à Sandy Lane (Saint-Jaques)
Strand bei Sandy Lane (St. James)
Playa en Sandy Lane (St. James)

Governor General's House
Le Palais gouvernemental
Haus des General-Statthalters
Palacio del Gobierno

South Point Lighthouse
Le Phare de South Point
Der South-Point-
Leuchtturm
Faro de South Point

Public Buildings, Trafalgar Square
Bâtiments administratifs à Trafalgar Square
Staatliche Gebäude am Trafalgar Square
Edificios públicos en la plaza de Trafálgar

Harbor Policeman,
Bridgetown

Agent de police dans le port
de Bridgetown

Hafenpolizist in Bridgetown

Policía portuario
en Bridgetown

Tropical Vegetation
in St. James (Miramar)
Végétation tropicale
à Saint-Jacques (Miramar)
Tropische Pflanzenwelt
in St. James (Miramar)
Vegetación tropical
en St. James (Miramar)

Crane Beach

Morgan Lewis Sugar Plantation
La plantation de cannes à sucre Morgan Lewis
Die Morgan-Lewis-Zuckerrohrplantage
Plantación de caña de azúcar en Morgan Lewis

*Lord Nelson's Statue
on Trafalgar Square*

*La statue de Lord Nelson
à Trafalgar Square*

*Lord-Nelson-Denkmal
auf dem Trafalgar-Square*

*Estatua de Lord Nelson
en la plaza de Trafálgar*

Codrington College
Le collège de Codrington
Codrington Hochschule
Colegio de Codrington

Sunset on Carlisle Bay
Coucher de soleil sur la baie de Carlisle
Sonnenuntergang an der Carlisle-Bucht
Puesta de sol en la bahía de Carlisle

The center of this resort coast is Holetown, or St. James. One of the oldest churches in the West Indies, built in 1684, is here, and an obelisk that marks the spot where Captain Powell set foot in 1625.

Other noteworthy tourist spots worth visiting are St. George's Church, which houses the famous painting of the Resurrection by Benjamin West (1786); Welchman Hall Gully, Morgan Lewis Plantation, and Cherry Tree Hill.

Returning from the tour of the island, you approach Bridgetown through the resort sections of Hastings, Worthing, and St. Lawrence, which will remind you of the English Sussex Coast. Christ Church is the scene of the famous nineteenth-century Barbados Coffin Mystery, in which the coffins in a vault were disturbed in a variety of ways through no explicable means more than a hundred years ago. Tourists in search of every interesting facet of an island still make a beeline to "Chase's Vault," although it has been empty for generations.

BARBADOS — THE PEOPLE

Barbadians, or Bajans, are famous throughout the Caribbean for their hospitality, gaiety, and charm. Quick to smile, ready to help and to please, the Bajan is the greatest asset to the island's tourist industry. The population is among the best educated in the West Indies and has produced many of the leaders in the movement for West Indian independence.

Barbados has a ring of beaches whose pink-white sands can be compared for softness with that of granulated sugar. East coast or west coast, the swimming is hard to beat. If you like to ride the breakers, try them on the windward Atlantic Coast.

On the west coast, Freshwater Bay, with its Paradise Beach, in the Parish of St. Michael, is aptly named. Curious "springs" appear in the sand, where underground reservoirs of fresh sheet water pressing against sea water cause the fresh water to rise to the surface. Hence, Freshwater Bay. Ruins of one of Barbados' old forts stand at the far end of the beach. Silver Sands is south of Seawell Airport in Christ Church Parish. The early Arawaks enjoyed bathing here. Silver sand dunes and a blue surf make this colorful beach an ideal picnic-and-bathing area. Crane Beach, the site of a hotel that is a favorite with Barbadians, is just four miles north of Seawell Airport. If you prefer to brave a turbulent but safe surf, these beach waters are for you.

Another lovely beach south of Crane is Foul Bay, while northward, toward Sam Lord's Castle and beyond to Edgewater Hotel and Kittredge's Bay, are found still more lovely beaches and isolated coves, some of which are planted with coconut trees. The largest of these is Long Bay, which is outstanding because of the surrounding cliffs.

On the west coast, north of Bridgetown, the Coral Reef Club, Sandy Lane, Paradise Beach, Miramar, Colony, Buccaneer Bay Apartment Hotel, Sattler's Beach, Coconut Creek, Greensleeve Apartel, Sunset Lodge, and Eastry House are superb resorts, with beaches whose waters are more tranquil than those on the east coast of Barbados. To the south are the St. Lawrence Hotel, the Caribbee, the Royal Caribbean, the Royal-on-Sea, the lively Blue Waters Beach Hotel, and Rockley Beach, the Windsor, Ocean View, Bonnie Dundee, Island Inn, Half Moon, Accra Beach, San Remo Beach, Bagshot House, Silver Beach, Aquatic Club, Sandy Beach, and South Winds, to name some of the best.

Inland, the stately Marine Hotel, with its magnificent swimming pool and gardens, is noted for its excellent Continental cuisine. It's the oldest hotel on the island, dating back to 1878.

On Needham's Point the new Barbados Hilton Hotel (with 150 rooms) overlooks Carlisle Bay. A new resort area has been started on the north end of the island with the North Point Surf Resort, which includes the largest swimming pool on Barbados. It is of Olympic size and contains half a million gallons of water.

Sailing is a favorite pastime, and since Barbados is, after all, an English island, horseback riding goes on everywhere.

Golf is played at a nine-hole course at Rockley Golf Club, three miles from Bridgetown, and at Sandy Lane (St. James). There are also four great spectator sports – cricket, horse racing, soccer, and polo. Race meets are held in the spring, summer, and fall on the Garrison Savannah near Bidgetown.

THE STATELY HOMES OF BARBADOS

Ilaro Court offers a fascinating view of the rolling hills and countryside around this splendid mansion, one of the more picturesque in Barbados.

Bay Mansion is a true Barbadian Great House. Parts of the building go back as far as 1750.

Drax Hall in St. George Parish is one of the finest examples of an early Barbadian Plantation House. It features an exceptionally fine staircase.

Colleton House in St. Peter's Parish is a onetime planter's home, typically well-preserved. A long drive lined with shade trees leads to the house, terminating at a fountain. The house offers a panoramic view of St. Peter's coastline.

Nicholas Abbey is one of the few Barbadian mansions to have more than one fireplace. This house and Drax Hall are considered to be the oldest houses in Barbados.

Alleynedale House in St. Lucy Parish was built, it is believed, by the same architect who constructed Nicholas Abbey. Formerly owned by the Tyrell family, the last member of which committed suicide and lies buried in the cellar, the house is said to be haunted by his restless ghost.

Governor General's House in Bridgetown is occupied by the British sovereign's representative in Barbados. The grounds are beautifully laid out and the interiors are handsome and spacious. High ceilings from which hang lovely glass chandeliers, and wide decorative arches leading into smaller rooms, are features of the traditional Barbadian Mansion.

Acknowledgment

My appreciation goes to the Department of External Affairs of Barbados for supplying me with information on the background of the island's independence.

In setting up the final picture selection for this book, I had the kind assistance of Frank J. Odle and Noel Smith. Paul Foster assisted in the description of certain pictures, and Jimmy (E. L.) Cozier rechecked my copy from the island's viewpoint. May I thank them and T. O'Conor Sloane III, editor, Doubleday & Company, Inc., who extended his assistance to me in a final checkup of the whole book.

Hans Hannau

THE PLATES

On Carlisle Bay

This view from the Royal Barbados Yacht Club gives an idea of the busy traffic in Carlisle Bay and in the harbor of Bridgetown; large and small vessels come and go: large cruise ships ply their way to the new deep-water harbor north of Bridgetown, and freighters, sailboats, and elegant yachts are plentiful.

Old Sugar Mill

Ruins of old sugar mills are found all over Barbados, standing among extensive fields of sugar cane, the production of which is one of the island's main industries. In the foreground is a blooming frangipani tree with its beautiful red flowers. Frangipani trees are plentiful on Barbados.

Bridgetown, The Careenage

One of the landmarks of Barbados is this colorful inlet with its busy wharfs where, for over 300 years, ships of all makes and origins have docked for overhauling, cleaning, and calking. The scene is changing fast: old buildings are replaced by new ones, and in a few years it will all be very different. This is one of the most picturesque points in the Caribbean.

Secluded Beach on the Caribbean Coast (Eastry House)

In contrast to busy Bridgetown, the stretches of beach north of the city along St. Michael's, St. James's, and St. Peter's parishes are quiet and relaxing, a paradise for vacationers. Some of the finest resorts on the island are found here – Coral Reef, Sandy Lane, Eastry House, Miramar, Paradise Beach, Sunset Lodge, and Colony Club. The picture shows the beautiful secluded beach connected with Eastry House.

Bridgetown

This air view of the center of the capital of Barbados shows most clearly the old-world charm of this interesting city. The Careenage is visible as well as the government buildings, St. Michael's Cathedral, and, in the background, the sugar-cane fields and hills. Bridgetown was established about 1629 and was named after an Indian bridge that crossed the Careenage. The city has today approximately 96,000 inhabitants.

St. James Coast at Coral Reef Club

Great vacation days are spent among the beautiful resorts along the St. James coast. Sailing, fishing, swimming, water skiing, snorkeling, and boating are some of the many sports offered to the tourist on Barbados' "Platinum Coast." In the background is the renowned Coral Reef Club with its beautiful beach.

Welchman's Hall Gully

In the very center of the island at St. Thomas is this paradise valley of tropical plants and trees.

Sam Lord's Castle

This is one of the show places of Barbados. Approximately fifteen miles from Bridgetown, it was built in 1820 by Sam Lord at Long Bay on the Atlantic Coast. Many a tale has been written about this famous site – how Sam Lord fixed lanterns in the coconut trees which caused ships passing in the night to think there was a harbor where in fact there was nothing but coral reefs, upon which the unfortunate vessels were dashed. And thus Sam Lord salvaged valuable cargos, enabling him to build one of the most luxurious homes on the island, now an outstanding resort. Sam Lord died in London in 1845.

Garrison Race Track

At the south end of Bridgetown is Garrison Savannah with its famous race track. Horse racing is one of the many spectator sports offered in Barbados. There are three annual meetings of four days each in March, August, and November at the "Garrison" – a big event for all of Barbados.

The old Harbor of Speightstown (St. Peter's)

Speightstown is the second most important town in Barbados, after Bridgetown, and is a center of the island's fishing industry. It has lovely parks, a library, banks, and an impressive old harbor, shown in the picture. In the past, the harbor had a brisk trade going with Bristol, England, and there was daily schooner service to Bridgetown. The town derives its name from William Speight, who at one time owned the grounds on which the town was built.

St. Michael's Cathedral, Bridgetown

Originally a parish church, St. Michael's became a cathedral in 1824. The first St. Michael's Church on this location was consecrated in 1665 and destroyed by a hurricane in 1780. The present church, built in 1789, was damaged by a hurricane in 1831. It is a cathedral of the Church of England, and its clergy is paid by the state. Interesting tombstones going back to the seventeenth century can be found here.

Atlantic Coast at Bathsheba

The rocky Atlantic coast, with fine sandy beaches between the picturesque rock formations, has its own charm and atmosphere. The picture shows such a beach near the Edgewater Hotel, visible on top of the rocks.

Sugar-Cane Fields on the Eastern Slopes from Cherry Tree Hill

Looking over the fertile slopes from a hill down to the Atlantic Coast, this picture reproduces a peaceful scene that is typical of Barbados.

Rockley Golf Course

Located in the Parish of Christchurch, this excellent standard nine-hole golf course is popular with vacationers. Another attractive course, at the Sandy Lane Golf Club (St. James's

Parish), belongs to the elegant Sandy Lane Hotel.

Paradise Beach at Freshwater Bay (St. James)

This beautiful beach stretches before one of the island's best resorts (Paradise Beach Hotel) and is noted for its very interesting phenomenon: several fresh-water springs break out along the beach, giving its name to Freshwater Bay. Rare birds are found in the casuarina trees along the beach, among them the beautiful Golden Warbler.

Barbados International Airport and the Police Force

Barbados' modern Seawell Airport, close to the southeastern (Atlantic) coast, is the place where the Princess Royal Alice was greeted by the is-

land's elegant police force. Princess Alice is seen walking past the lines.

The Marine Hotel, a Historic Landmark

This hotel, erected in 1879, was responsible for starting Barbados' important tourist industry. Although it is not situated directly on the ocean, it has a beautiful swimming pool, terrace, and large gardens. There is an excellent cuisine, and many of the rooms are air-conditioned. It is a popular hotel with modern comforts.

North Point near Animal Flower Cave

In the northwestern part of the island (St. Lucy) where white waters storm against the cliffs and carve out caves of unusual form along the rocky coast, there is a large underground cave studded with "animal flowers," colorful sea-anemones that look like red, yellow, and pink flowers. There are also interesting stalagmite and stalactite formations. A visit to these caves is well worthwhile.

St. Martin's Church

Close to Sam Lord's Castle in St. Philip is this picturesque church, seen through a curtain of frangipani flowers. The little island of Barbados has more than seventy churches, mostly old, historic, and Anglican, with interesting architectural features.

Pico Teneriffe

This attractive scene is on the eastern coast of the most northern parish of St. Lucy, on the borderline of St. Peter's Parish.

Beach at Sandy Lane (St. James)

Sandy Lane is in the heart of St. James' Parish, which is the "Platinum Coast" of Barbados. The magnificent resort, built in 1961, lies directly on the beautiful beach shown in the picture. Every modern convenience and resort feature, including a nine-hole golf course, is found here.

Governor General's House

This dignified old building, which for more than 250 years has been the residence of the island's governors, has been the site of most important diplomatic receptions. Queen Elizabeth, Princess Margaret, and the Princess Royal Alice were fêted here by Governor Sir John Stow. It is a delightfully old-fashioned Barbadian mansion, with beautiful gardens.

South Point Lighthouse

Many lighthouses surround Barbados, because of the busy ship traffic. The picture shows the lighthouse close to the airport on the south point of the island.

Public Buildings, Trafalgar Square

From Chamberlain Bridge over the open spaces of Trafalgar Square, the attractive public buildings catch the eye. Built in 1874, they are in elegant Renaissance style, with an inner court where the Chambers of the House of Assembly and the Post Office are located.

Harbor Policeman, Bridgetown

The harbor police, with their unusual uniform (similar to that worn by the water police on the Thames), have become a symbol of Barbados. Doing duty in the morning along the harbor facilities in Bridgetown, the police are popular subjects of photography by tourists.

Tropical Vegetation in St. James (Miramar)

This majestic row of Royal Palms is part of the tropical grounds of a beautiful resort. The Miramar Beach Hotel, directly on the beach of St. James, has a large swimming pool, terrace, and elegant modern buildings.

Crane Beach

The Barbadians, as well as visitors from other places, are fond of Crane Beach on the southeastern Atlantic coast of Barbados, not far from the airport. One of the island's best beaches, it is beautifully situated, with a small hotel on top of a rock (background). This is the Crane Hotel, which has seventeen guest rooms. Meals are served on a terrace.

Morgan Lewis Sugar Plantation

This is one of the very old plantations still profitably growing sugar cane. The old sugar mill – clearly visible in the picture – was an important background shot in the film "Island in the Sun." Barbados maintains its historic appearance through the Barbados National Trust, an organization created for the purpose of preserving historic buildings, monuments, forts, and points of natural beauty. Sugar is still the leading income-producing commodity of the island. More than 90,000 acres are dedicated to sugar-cane production.

Peasant Home

One of the most noteworthy features of Barbados is its cleanliness. Streets, buildings, and even the homes of the peasantry are kept clean and tidy. Simply constructed – at times only a corrugated sheet is used for a roof – these homes are kept in perfect shape, and beautified with flowerbeds.

Lord Nelson's Statue on Trafalgar Square

Sir Richard Westmacott's statue of Lord Nelson overlooks the expanse of Trafalgar Square. Lord Nelson was responsible for breaking Napoleon's sea power, which was endangering Barbados. This was the first monument erected in honor of the great Admiral. The inscription reads as follows:
To the memory of Horatio Lord Viscount Nelson, K. B., the Pre-

server of the British West Indies in a moment of unexampled peril ... this statue was erected by the grateful inhabitants of Barbados ... February 24th A. D. 1813.
Esto Perpetua!

Codrington College

Christopher Codrington, founder of this seminary, was born in Barbados in 1668. In 1700 he became governor of the Leeward Islands, retiring to Barbados in 1707, where he died on Good Friday, April 7, 1710. He left his two sugar estates to the Society for the Propagation of the Gospel, in London, to be used for the founding of a college for the study of religion and medicine, under vows of chastity, poverty, and obedience, on the lines of a monastic order. Anglican priests of the Community of the Resurrection in Mirfield (Yorkshire) keep up this work in affiliation with the University of Durham (England).

Sunset on Carlisle Bay

A magnificent sunset colors the sky and the clear waters of Carlisle Bay in brilliant red and orange. Carlisle Bay is on the Caribbean coast of Barbados, with Bridgetown in the center. To the north lies a small peninsula (really a small island, called Pelican Island) alongside one of the finest deep-water harbors to be found in the West Indies. Finished in 1961, it boasts excellent harbor facilities and an Industrial Park. To the south, Carlisle Bay follows a peninsula on whose tip stands Barbados' newest and largest hotel, the Barbados Hilton, overlooking beautiful gardens, an attractive beach, the ever-changing hues of the bay with its many boats lying in anchorage, and the city of Bridgetown in the background.

PANORAMA-BOOKS

USA: Arizona* · California · California Missions · Cape Cod · Florida · Los Angeles · Michigan* · New York · San Francisco · Virginia · Washington D. C. Yosemite

Caribbean: Barbados · Guadeloupe · Jamaica · Martinique · Nassau · Puerto Rico Trinidad & Tobago · The Virgin Islands

Germany: Bavaria · Bavarian Alps · Bavarian Royal Castles · Berlin · The Black Forest · Bonn · Cologne · Essen · Hamburg · Heidelberg · Lake Constance Moselle · Munich · The Rhine · Romantic Germany · The Ruhr

Austria: Austria · Badgastein · Carinthia · Salzburg and Surroundings · Styria Tyrol · Vienna

France: Alsace · Brittany · Châteaux of the Loire · Corsica · Côte d'Azur · French Cathedrals · Mont Saint-Michel · Normandy · Paris · Paris by Night · Provence

Italy: Capri · Florence · The Gulf of Naples · Pompeii · Rome · Sicily · Southern Tyrol · Venice

Scandinavia: Copenhagen · Denmark · Finland · Helsinki · Lapland · Norway Sweden

Switzerland: Grisons · Lake Geneva · Lake Lucerne · Romantic Switzerland Switzerland

Capitals of the world: Athens · Brasilia · Brussels · Istanbul · London · Moscow Peking · Rio de Janeiro

Other countries: Andalusia · Balearic Islands · Bermuda · Canada · Costa del Sol Canary Islands · Flanders · Greece · The Holy Land · Ireland · Israel · Japan Mexico · Morocco · New Zealand · The Netherlands · Portugal · Rhodes · Scotland Spain · Yugoslavia – Dalmatian Coast

* In preparation   EDITOR HANS ANDERMANN